MW01094503

PAUL
Proclaiming Christ Crucified

Ronald D. Witherup

Little Rock
Scripture Study

*A ministry of the Diocese of Little Rock
in partnership with Liturgical Press*

Nihil obstat: Jerome Kodell, O.S.B., *Censor Librorum.*
Imprimatur: ✝ Anthony B. Taylor, Bishop of Little Rock, June 30, 2016.

Cover design by Ann Blattner. Cover photo: Lightstock. Used with permission.

Photos/illustrations: Page 6, cross, window at Saint Stephen's Church, Anoka, Minnesota. Photo by Gene Plaisted, OSC © The Crosiers. Used with permission. Page 10, *Eleventh Station* from Saint Peter Canisius Church, Nijmegen, Netherlands. Photo by Gene Plaisted, OSC © The Crosiers. Used with permission. Pages 12, 24, 28 (ancient baptismal font), 33, 34, 36 (olive tree), and 39, Thinkstock Images by Getty. Used with permission. Page 14, *Christ*, folk art by Lars Christianson, Norwegian-American Museum, Decorah, Iowa. Photo by Gene Plaisted, OSC © The Crosiers. Used with permission. Page 18, *Crucifix* from Saint Peter's, Brighton, UK. Photo by Gene Plaisted, OSC © The Crosiers. Used with permission.

ISBN: 978-0-8146-3693-0 (print); 978-0-8146-3694-7 (ebook)

Contents

Introduction

Alive in the Word brings you resources to deepen your understanding of Scripture, offer meaning for your life today, and help you to pray and act in response to God's word.

Use any volume of **Alive in the Word** in the way best suited to you.

- **For individual learning and reflection,** consider this an invitation to prayerfully journal in response to the questions you find along the way. And be prepared to move from head to heart and then to action.
- **For group learning and reflection,** arrange for three sessions where you will use the material provided as the basis for faith sharing and prayer. You may ask group members to read each chapter in advance and come prepared with questions answered. In this kind of session, plan to be together for about an hour. Or, if your group prefers, read and respond to the questions together without advance preparation. With this approach, it's helpful to plan on spending more time for each group session in order to adequately work through each chapter.

- **For a parish-wide event** or use within a larger group, provide each person with a copy of this volume, and allow time during the event for quiet reading, group discussion and prayer, and then a final commitment by each person to some simple action in response to what he or she learned.

This volume explores a key theme in Paul's writings and is one of several volumes dedicated to the **Cloud of Witnesses** theme. The pages of our Bibles are filled with the stories of women and men who have played a unique role in salvation history. By entering into a few key biblical passages written by or describing these people, we begin to see how our own story continues God's great work of salvation in the world. Their witness, handed on to us from centuries ago, continues to speak to us and challenge us to stand as faithful witnesses in today's world.

The Wisdom of the Cross

Begin by asking God to assist you in your prayer and study. Then read through 1 Corinthians 1:18-25 slowly, a passage on the special wisdom of the cross.

1 Corinthians 1:18-25
[18]The message of the cross is foolishness to those who are perishing, but to us who are being saved it is the power of God. [19]For it is written:

"I will destroy the wisdom of the wise, and the learning of the learned I will set aside."

[20]Where is the wise one? Where is the scribe? Where is the debater of this age? Has not God made the wisdom of the world foolish? [21]For since in the wisdom of God the world did not come to know God through wisdom, it was the will of God through the foolishness of the proclamation to save those who have faith. [22]For Jews demand signs and Greeks look for wisdom, [23]but we proclaim Christ crucified, a stumbling block to Jews and foolishness to Gentiles, [24]but to those who are called, Jews and Greeks alike, Christ the power of God and the wisdom of God. [25]For the foolishness of God is

wiser than human wisdom, and the weakness of
God is stronger than human strength.

*After a few minutes of quiet reflection
on the passage, consider the information
provided in "Setting the Scene."*

Setting the Scene

Unlike the four Gospels, the apostle Paul did
not tell stories about Jesus of Nazareth. Rather,
he wrote letters to multiple faith communities
throughout the ancient Mediterranean basin to
explain to them the significance of Jesus Christ,
that is, Jesus Messiah, the Anointed One of God.
Yet behind these letters, indeed, stands a
powerful narrative, especially about the cross,
death, and resurrection of Jesus Christ and what
all these mean for the salvation of the world.

Paul of Tarsus, who became known as "the
Apostle to the Gentiles" (Acts 9:15; Gal 2:7-9),
was a missionary, evangelizer, and founder of
Christian communities. He is also Christianity's
foremost letter-writer, with thirteen letters of the
New Testament bearing his name. Although he
never knew Jesus of Nazareth in the flesh, and
indeed had persecuted the Church (see Gal 1:13),
the risen Lord Jesus called him to become an
"apostle," one sent on a mission (see Acts 9:1-19
and Gal 1:15-16).

The present passage concerns the wisdom of
the cross. It occurs in the first chapter of the First
Letter of Paul to the Corinthians where Paul
strongly reminds them that the cross is central
to the faith. Paul had founded the Corinthian

Have you ever
experienced
divisions or
factions in your
parish or
community?
What effect did
they have? Were
there ways to
overcome them?

community, where he spent considerable time in ministry and earning money as a tentmaker (see Acts 18:1-4). He wrote this letter to them around AD 53–54 from Ephesus (in modern-day western Turkey), after getting reports "from Chloe's people" of difficulties in the community (1:11). A primary problem among the Corinthians—one that has sadly been repeated many times throughout Christian history—was the existence of factions (1:10-17). Members, we might say, had "fan clubs." Some favored one minister over another, with the result that fractious divisions were developing contrary to the ideal unity of Christian fellowship.

Paul also used the occasion of his letter to answer a number of questions that the Corinthians had asked him about in an earlier letter (7:1). These matters were largely ethical questions, which Paul addresses by citing Christian tradition that he himself had received, such as the traditions of the Last Supper (11:23-26) and the resurrection of the dead (15:1-8), or some of his own teaching (7:12).

This remarkable "pastoral" letter, then, is Paul's attempt to deal in a straightforward manner with multiple kinds of community problems in the church. Yet the way in which he chooses to address them is highly theological, rooted in his understanding of the unique wisdom of the cross of Christ.

What ways do you think can promote better community life?

How do you participate in evangelization? In what ways do you take the opportunity to share the "good news" of the Gospel of Jesus Christ?

Understanding the Scene

[18]The message of the cross is foolishness to those who are perishing, but to us who are being saved it is the power of God. [19]For it is written:
"I will destroy the wisdom of the wise, and the learning of the learned I will set aside."

Recall the context as you begin this passage. Divisions have marked the Corinthian community. People have gravitated to different leaders, especially those who baptized them (Paul himself; Apollos, a respected figure in Corinth; Kephas [Simon Peter, Jesus' foremost apostle]; and even Christ, as if he were a separate leader). Paul reminds the Corinthians that baptism was not his primary ministry; rather, he was "to preach the gospel, and not with the wisdom of human eloquence, so that the cross of Christ might not be emptied of its meaning" (1 Cor 1:17).

So the setup for our passage is Paul calling the Corinthians back to a foundational insight. In light of their petty squabbles over whom to follow, Paul sends them to the cross. In essence, Paul is reminding the Corinthians to return to a foremost essential of the Christian faith.

The challenge, however, is that the cross was an offensive symbol in the dual cultural worlds in which Paul lived. The entire passage is

How do you feel about making the sign of the cross in public? Is it indeed a sign of your own faith?

imprinted with allusions to both the secular Greco-Roman world and the religious milieu of Judaism. Paul admits a dualistic reaction to the cross; it is folly or wisdom. The cross was, in fact, a most feared and despised symbol of

the Roman Empire's domination of Paul's world. It was considered so cruel that the Romans did not permit its use on Roman citizens. Crucifixion was a hideous, extremely painful, and humiliating death reserved to enemies of the state or escaped slaves. It was preceded by scourging and other tortures, culminating in being nailed or bound to a cross, usually naked, exposed to the elements and the mocking gaze of onlookers.

Despite the horror of the cross, Paul offers another perspective. He admits that some (those who are perishing) see it as foolishness (the Greek word *mōria*, from which we get "moron"). But others (those being saved; thus, people of faith) see it as evidence of "the power of God."

For many people, the cross has become a kind of trinket or merely a piece of jewelry to wear. How do you view such developments? Are there ways to make the cross more meaningful today?

The message of the cross is thus deeply paradoxical. When you gaze upon it, depending on your perspective, you can see it as utter folly and defeat, or you can view it as strangely powerful—with the ability to save. Paul later writes to the Corinthians of his deep insight that weakness, in the eyes of faith, is actually a form of power (2 Cor 12:6-10). This is a recollection of the "message of the cross."

Paul caps his image with a quotation from Scripture, from the prophet Isaiah (19:14). (Note well: Paul frequently went to the Sacred Scriptures, the Greek version of the Old Testament, for God's message, just as you are doing). The prophet's words occur in the context of God urging the kingdom of Judah not to plead for Egyptian military assistance in the face of Assyrian aggression. In poetic language, the prophet's words say that God will destroy human wisdom and learning. They count for nothing in the eyes of faith. Real power does not derive from military might or strategy. It comes from steadfast faith in God alone. Paul uses the passage to bolster his message that real power lies in the cross of Christ.

> *Real power comes from steadfast faith in God alone.*

[20]**Where is the wise one? Where is the scribe? Where is the debater of this age? Has not God made the wisdom of the world foolish?** [21]**For since in the wisdom of God the world did not come to know God through wisdom, it was the will of God through the foolishness of the proclamation to save those who have faith.**

Paul then turns from power to wisdom and learning. He begins with four rhetorical questions, adding a comment in response. His language subtly addresses both the Greco-Roman world and the Jewish world of his day. The image of the wise one (Greek *sophos*) recalls the Greeks' admiration of philosophy (literally, "love of wisdom"). They placed confidence in human reason, and they exalted philosophers whom they considered wise. In Paul's day, multiple Greek philosophies vied for the public's attention. Philosophers made all sorts of claims and offered many kinds of supposed "knowledge" that could enable people to maneuver in a complex and cruel world. Paul dismisses such folly (a verb related to *mōria*!), asserting that true wisdom is found elsewhere.

On the Jewish side of Paul's argument is the image of the scribe. More than simply one with

the ability to read and write, the scribe in Judaism was considered an expert in the Torah, God's law, which the scribes preserved and interpreted. They were considered real experts, authentic interpreters of the law of Moses. Again, Paul dismisses such an understanding with his rhetorical question.

The third question, on the "debater of this age," refers to those with expertise in argumentation. It employs a rare Greek word that usually has a pejorative meaning: someone who likes to provoke disputes just for the sake of argumentation. The statement following the three questions reveals how Paul views all three images: they represent the foolish wisdom of the world, not God's true wisdom.

We may like rational thinking, human wisdom, legal wrangling, or sharp debates, but one does not find a truly divine perspective in such purely human endeavors. Paul alludes to the ability to know God through reason but, he says, humans did not ultimately use it properly to know God (v. 21). Rather, he claims that a type of "foolishness" (*mōria* again) leads to true salvation, the nature of which he explains in the next section.

²²For Jews demand signs and Greeks look for wisdom, ²³but we proclaim Christ crucified, a stumbling block to Jews and foolishness to Gentiles, ²⁴but to those who are called, Jews and Greeks alike, Christ the power of God and the wisdom of God. ²⁵For the foolishness of God is wiser than human wisdom, and the weakness of God is stronger than human strength.

Now comes Paul's explanation of his own position, intended to bring the Corinthians to their senses. The problem is that both principal cultures of Paul's day were looking for power and wisdom in the wrong places. (Are we so different today?) He says bluntly, "Jews demand signs and Greeks look for wisdom." From the perspective of faith, neither is effective.

Paradoxically, the message "we proclaim" (using the classic Christian word for preaching, *kērysso*) is "Christ crucified." This expression invokes the image of a crucifix, not simply a cross. One gazes upon Christ physically on the cross as a paradoxical symbol of power and wisdom. In the eyes of the world, this is an absurdity. How could a humiliated, defeated, bloodied, crucified man be a source of power and wisdom? Paul freely admits the image makes no sense in rational, human terms. It is a "stumbling block" (*skandolon*, from which comes our word "scandal") to Jews and "foolishness" (*mōria* once more) to Gentiles. It makes no rational sense.

But Paul then makes sense out of his assertions through the eyes of faith. "[T]o those who are called" refers to the community of faith. We are "the elect," (*klētois*, the called or chosen, from the same Greek root as *ekklēsia*, "church") those whom God has *called* to faith, whether Gentile or Jew. Thus, we see and interpret reality differently from those whose only perspective is the worldly sphere. Interestingly, Paul does not really complete his sentence. Note that there is no verb in verse 24. Paul simply lets the expression conclude his thought: "Christ the power of God and the wisdom of God." It is as if no verb is necessary. One simply gazes upon Christ crucified.

Then Paul explains what this means in human terms. Despite appearances, Christ crucified in fact means that the "foolishness" of God is far wiser than any human wisdom, and the "weakness" of God is far stronger than any human strength. Such a profound paradox! For most human beings, power and wisdom lie in being literally strong, well-armed, aggressive, dominating, and shrewd. But in Christian terms, Paul claims that true power and wisdom are found in vulnerability and offering one's life for others, just as Christ died for the world. That is the wisdom and power of the cross.

What do you think of Paul's description of foolishness and wisdom? How realistic is it?

Praying the Word / Sacred Reading

Place before you an image of the crucified Christ, whether a painting or a crucifix, and sit quietly before it, meditating upon it. Use your imagination to experience vicariously that day when Christ was crucified, died, and was buried. What would it have been like to be a witness to the crucifixion? What part might you have played in the passion story? What role would you have fulfilled? A curious bystander? A Roman soldier? A fearful disciple who fled? One of the faithful women who watched from a distance?

At the end of your meditation, you might consider journaling your experience or perhaps pray the following prayer (or create your own).

How would you explain the message of the cross to a non-Christian?

Oh, Jesus, my crucified Savior! Teach me the wisdom of the cross. How I wish I could learn from you what it means to be powerful in weakness, to be victorious in giving up all!

I can scarcely imagine the suffering you underwent, and I am not sure that I could endure it. Give me some small share in your ability to accept suffering without complaint, and to willingly offer myself for the sake of others.

Teach me, Lord, the power of the cross—what it means to surrender my all in order that I might gain even more by your love.

When I am tempted to argue or to debate with others, Lord, teach me humility. Let me not succumb to having to always win, to try to conquer others, or to bully them to accept my way. Let me learn to humbly follow the way of the cross, as you did, so that I might share in your own suffering in order to share in your new life.

Let me never be scandalized or ashamed, Lord, by the cross or by my faith. Strengthen my resolve so that I might more worthily proclaim the message of the cross and resurrection. Help me to build up the community of faith in humility and not damage it by my pride. May all that I do bring glory to your name! I pray this humbly with the aid of your Holy Spirit and to the glory of your heavenly Father. Amen.

Living the Word

Consider concrete ways to promote more unity in your parish, your faith community, or even your family. What can you do to bring people closer together? An evening of refreshments and sharing? A meal together? A Bible sharing session using an appropriate passage on the cross of Christ?

The Glory of the Cross

Begin by asking God to assist you in your prayer and study. Then read through Philippians 2:5-11 slowly, which speaks of the glory of the cross.

Philippians 2:5-11
[5]Have among yourselves the same attitude that is also yours in Christ Jesus,
[6]Who, though he was in the form of God,
did not regard equality with God something to be grasped.
[7]Rather, he emptied himself, taking the form of a slave, coming in human likeness; and found human in appearance,
[8]he humbled himself,
becoming obedient to death, even death on a cross.
[9]Because of this, God greatly exalted him
and bestowed on him the name
that is above every name,

¹⁰that at the name of Jesus
every knee should bend,
of those in heaven and on earth and under the
    earth,
¹¹and every tongue confess that
Jesus Christ is Lord,
to the glory of God the Father.

*After a few minutes of quiet reflection
on the passage, consider the information
provided in "Setting the Scene."*

Setting the Scene

Paul's Letter to the Philippians, short though it is, is one of Paul's most memorable letters, written during an imprisonment, perhaps this time in Rome. Not only does it offer some auto-biographical information about Paul's background and that of some of his colleagues (see 2:19-30; 3:4b-11), but it also resounds with the vocabulary of "joy" (the noun "joy" and various forms of the verb "rejoice")—a bit ironic, given his captivity.

What challenges you most in finding joy in the midst of difficult situations? How can you better bring a joyful attitude to your life even on days when things are simply not going as well as you would like?

The main purpose of the letter is to thank the Philippians for their financial and other assistance, and also to commend to them one of Paul's ministerial colleagues, Epaphroditus, who had brought him Philippian aid but then had fallen seriously ill. Paul sends him back earlier than expected to his native Philippi in order to alleviate their anxiety (2:25-28). Paul tenderly calls him "my brother and co-worker and fellow soldier" (2:25). Paul also uses the occasion to underline the importance of maintaining fellowship or partnership within the community, as well as with him at a distance during his imprisonment (1:5-7).

One can tell visually from the form of the text (2:5-11) that it is a poetic passage. The content also reveals it to be a christological hymn, that is, it honors Jesus Christ. This "hymn" (or poem, really) is not only the guiding image of the whole letter, but some scholars find it to be the overarching image for Paul's message. One might consider it the gospel in miniature, the story of Jesus from his preexistence with the Father in heaven, to his descent to earth to suffer and die on the cross, to his vindication in the resurrection and ascension back to the Father. Whether Paul inherited it from earlier Christian tradition, and then modified it somewhat, or composed it himself, is not certain. What is certain is that its rich poetic vision has inspired countless generations of Christians through the ages.

Do you know anyone whose attitudes and/or behavior you would like to emulate? How easy or difficult is it to adopt someone else's attitudes while keeping your own unique identity?

Hundreds of volumes have been written about this poem, traditionally called in Latin *Carmen Christi* (literally, "the song of Christ"). It is also called the "kenotic hymn" (from Greek *ekenōsen*, "emptied himself"; v. 7), indicating the self-sacrificing example provided by Christ. In the context of the letter, Paul presents it as *the* model of Christian behavior. Paul here is not speaking of Jesus of Nazareth in his activity of teaching and miracles, but Christ Jesus in his attitude of humility and self-sacrifice exemplified by his suffering and death on the cross. Indeed, the four verses that lead into this hymn speak strongly of the need for unity and humility in the community (2:1-4).

As with the Corinthian community, the Philippians were also bothered by divisions (lack of unity is such a human experience!). Paul urges them not to be selfish but humble, not to seek their own interests but the good of others. This leads him to propose Christ as the perfect model for Christian behavior, and the "attitude" that should be evident in the life of the community itself.

There are different ways to outline the hymn (e.g., 2, 3, or 4 stanzas) but its basic movement progresses from the incarnation—Christ taking on human flesh—to his exaltation in glory, passing through the experience of death, even the humiliating and excruciating death by crucifixion. Paul's powerful theology of the cross is in view. It is a dominant image, but the cross itself is not the final word. Ultimately, Christ's suffering and death on the cross led to his vindication by God, the Father. Exaltation here represents the resurrection/ascension. Christ's death is but a passage to a new life in which all who share in faith by baptism partake. Paul uses this image to great effect, reminding the Philippians of the need to maintain a joyful attitude in the midst of community sufferings, and to make personal sacrifices for the sake of others.

We will consider the entire passage a few verses at a time. The occasional questions in the margin (as above) are there for discussion with others or for personal reflection or journaling.

Understanding the Scene

⁵Have among yourselves the same attitude that
   is also yours in Christ Jesus,
⁶Who, though he was in the form of God,
did not regard equality with God something to
   be grasped.

The hymn begins with an imperative form of the Greek verb "to think, to form an opinion, to adopt a mentality" (*phroneō*). The NRSV translation captures the sense well: "Let the same mind be in you that was in Christ Jesus" (v. 5). The word really means more than simply imitate Christ Jesus; it means to adopt the same mindset, to incorporate the same attitudes as were found in Christ Jesus. Elsewhere Paul affirms a similar idea when he says "we have the mind of Christ." Adopting Christ's self-effacing attitude is not impossible. In fact, Paul views it as necessary.

How well do you feel that you imitate the mindset of the Lord Jesus? Do you accept suffering without complaint? Can you maintain joy in the midst of suffering?

The next verse begins the hymn proper, which consists of a series of short, pithy statements. It begins with an assertion that Christ was in the "form of God" (*morphē theou*). This phrase has occasioned considerable scholarly debate. The expression usually means "outward appearance" or "shape" or "form." Is it perhaps referring to Christ's preexistence with God? This is not absolutely clear, but the next verse helps clarify that equal status to God is implied.

Despite his divine status, he did not regard this "equality" something "to be grasped." Christ's identity is equal to God's; he already possessed this identity. Yet he did not regard it as something to be held onto or "grasped," or as the NRSV translates, "exploited." In other words, Christ did possess this equal identity with God, but he had no desire to use it for his own ends. This attitude, in fact, can be recalled in the crucifixion scenes of the Synoptic Gospels, where Jesus is mocked by passersby to use his powers to save *himself* (Mark 15:29-32; Matt 27:39-43; Luke 23:35-37). Jesus refuses this temptation; his act of self-sacrifice is for the good of others (Luke 22:20). This is the attitude Paul wants to emphasize to the Philippians.

> [7]Rather, he emptied himself,
> taking the form of a slave,
> coming in human likeness;
> and found human in appearance,
> [8]he humbled himself,
> becoming obedient to death,
> even death on a cross.

The hymn continues with a strong word ("Rather") to contrast Christ's divine status with his humble attitude. Instead of exploiting his divine status for his own welfare, Christ "emptied himself" (using *ekenōsen*, the word that gives the hymn its name, "kenotic"). This is an act of *self*-emptying. It is not a forced activity,

Christian mystics often mention the importance of self-emptying in order to be filled with God's grace and love. What in your own life could be "emptied" so that you would be able to receive more readily God's love? Do people consider you full of yourself or humble enough to receive from others?

something done under duress, but a voluntary surrendering of divine identity. This remarkable self-effacement is then explained by six phrases.

The first phrase contrasts the prior "form of God" with the voluntary assumption of the "form of a slave." The contrast could not be greater in Paul's world. Divine status was something accorded to the emperor, whom the Romans considered the "son of God" or a god himself; slaves were of the lowest status in the culture. So Paul here is saying that Christ voluntarily gave up divine status to assume the lowest identity possible, a slave, someone of no account, who was charged with menial duties.

The next two phrases offer redundant images in parallel fashion: coming in human likeness and found human in appearance. The emphasis is clearly on Christ's humanity (the Greek *anthrōpos* [human being], not *anēr* [man]). This is tantamount to the Letter to the Hebrews' assertion that Christ was like us in all things but sin (Heb 4:15). For Paul, Christ's assumption of our lowly state implies a total human existence.

The last three phrases go on to explain the nature of this self-emptying. Christ "humbled himself, becoming obedient to death, even death on a cross." The verb used for humbling (*tapeinoō*), which also means "to make oneself low," is the same word Paul uses of himself in Philippians, when he says in a more mundane way, "I know indeed how to live in humble circumstances" (Phil 4:12). More is meant here, though. This is a humbling unto death, even to the horrific death on a cross. These verses, then, clarify and expand the kind of humility Christ Jesus assumed and that Paul says should be the same among the Philippians.

Note, too, that the expression "obedient" to death alludes to the fact that, by his humility, Christ Jesus obeyed the will of his heavenly Father.

> [9]Because of this, God greatly exalted him
> and bestowed on him the name
> that is above every name,
> [10]that at the name of Jesus
> every knee should bend,
> of those in heaven and on earth and under the
>   earth,
> [11]and every tongue confess that
> Jesus Christ is Lord,
> to the glory of God the Father.

All that preceded this point in the hymn is the *reason* for what follows. "Because of this" leads to the turnaround or the vindication of Christ's actions. Because he freely accepted to do the will of his Father, he receives a reward. The Greek word indicates a kind of hyper-exaltation, an exaltation beyond all measure.

The hymn then explains in some detail the content of this divine exaltation. God bestows on Christ Jesus "the name that is above every name." Which name? In the Old Testament, God's name was so sacred that the Jews refused to speak it, instead using a roundabout expression ("the LORD"; Hebrew *adonai*) or simply

Christian faith emphasizes the true humanity of Christ, as well as his true divinity. How readily can you accept the Incarnation of Christ in his fully human identity? Does this make it harder or easier to accept that he is also Lord of the universe?

designating it "the name" (Hebrew *ha shēm*). The next phrase seemingly gives the answer because it affirms the "name of Jesus," which will cause every knee to bend. This seems correct, at first glance, because in the early church the name "Jesus" itself became a sacred name and, for a time, was the name used even in baptismal ceremonies (Acts 2:38; 3:6; 4:18; 9:27). But the hymn builds to a bigger climax.

> *Jesus Christ is LORD!*

The insertion of a modified citation from the prophet Isaiah (Isa 45:18-25) points toward the proper interpretation. The climax is that every knee should bend and every tongue proclaim that Jesus Christ is LORD! The Isaiah passage, in fact, is about the exalted name of God as LORD (Hebrew *adonai*; Greek *kyrios*). To bestow this name upon Jesus Christ is to proclaim him God. In other words, this exaltation has returned Christ Jesus to his original status as God's equal, with which the hymn had begun. The universal nature of this exaltation is further emphasized by the insertion of the three-level description of the universe as the ancients understood it: "in heaven and on earth and under the earth" (Gen 1:1–2:4; Exod 20:4). So no matter where one goes in the whole cosmos, all will proclaim that Jesus Christ is LORD.

As important as this exaltation is, however, note that the hymn ends in a further doxology (from the Greek expression for "giving glory"). All this is accomplished "to the glory of God the Father," the One to whom Jesus himself freely offered his obedience. Jesus does all to the glory

How ready are you to be obedient to God's will? Do you have difficulty discerning that will for you? Have you sought the assistance of someone (like a priest or spiritual advisor) who could help you discern God's will?

of his heavenly Father, which is exactly what Paul also invites the Philippians to do.

Praying the Word / Sacred Reading

An ancient form of prayer is reciting a simple mantra over and over again in a rhythmic fashion. Consider doing this using the sacred name of Jesus or the expression "Jesus is Lord." (There is also a simple, one-line hymn written by Sr. Suzanne Toolan, RSM, titled, "Jesus Christ: Yesterday, Today and Forever," which could be sung over and over.)

Another prayer activity could be to try your hand at composing a similar "hymn" or "poem" in your own words that speaks of the glory of the cross based upon Philippians 2.

Living the Word

Identify someone or some group that has heavy "crosses" to bear, perhaps someone who is ill, or lonely, recent immigrants, someone who has recently lost a loved one or who is perhaps homeless. Visit that person or group and spend some time offering your friendship and your faith-filled perspective. Make it an upbeat, joyful visit.

The Mystery of Baptism

Begin by asking God to assist you in your prayer and study. Then read through Romans 6:1-11 slowly, a passage that reflects on the mystery of baptism as sharing in Christ's death and resurrection.

Romans 6:1-11

¹What then shall we say? Shall we persist in sin that grace may abound? Of course not! ²How can we who died to sin yet live in it? ³Or are you unaware that we who were baptized into Christ Jesus were baptized into his death? ⁴We were indeed buried with him through baptism into death, so that, just as Christ was raised from the dead by the glory of the Father, we too might live in newness of life.

⁵For if we have grown into union with him through a death like his, we shall also be united with him in the resurrection. ⁶We know that our old self was crucified with him, so that our sinful body might be done away with, that we might no longer be in slavery to sin. ⁷For a dead person has been absolved from sin. ⁸If, then, we have died with Christ, we believe that we shall also live with him. ⁹We know that Christ, raised from the dead, dies no more; death no longer has power over him. ¹⁰As to his death, he died to sin once and for all; as to his life, he lives for God. ¹¹Consequently, you too must think of yourselves as [being] dead to sin and living for God in Christ Jesus.

> *After a few minutes of quiet reflection on the passage, consider the information provided in "Setting the Scene."*

Setting the Scene

Paul's Letter to the Romans is without doubt his masterpiece. It is one of the last, if not *the* last letter of Paul, written around AD 58 from Corinth, after years of pastoral experience of evangelizing and establishing churches—small faith communities, really—throughout the Mediterranean basin. The origins of the church in Rome are obscure, but ancient Christian tradition holds that Peter, the chief spokesman of the apostles, founded it during his own missionary activity. When Paul writes the letter, the Christian community is well established there. He writes to them ostensibly for three reasons:

- He intends to use Rome as a stopover on his way to further missionary activity in Spain (Rom 15:24, 28).
- He wishes to share with them his understanding of faith in Christ Jesus, and all that it means. He calls this a "spiritual gift so that you may be strengthened" (Rom 1:11).
- He wants to hear *their* understanding of the faith, so that they can "be mutually encouraged by one another's faith" (Rom 1:12).

Because Paul develops a long train of thought and detailed argumentation in Romans, it can be challenging for a casual reader to catch the force of what Paul is getting at in any given passage. Context is thus of utmost importance. In this case, we must recall that the precipitating problem for Paul in this section of Romans actually goes back to the statement Paul made a few verses earlier (Rom 5:20). There Paul explains the purpose of the Mosaic law:

> The law entered in so that transgression might increase but, *where sin increased, grace overflowed all the more*, so that, as sin reigned in death, grace also might reign through justification for eternal life through Jesus Christ our Lord. (Rom 5:20-21)

The italicized words point to the problem. Paul's statement seemingly leads to a dangerous conclusion. If the increase of sin allowed grace to increase, then why not keep on sinning? The more we sin, the more grace will abound. Or as Paul says earlier in the letter, doing evil so that some "good may come of it" (Rom 3:8). It sounds logical. Indeed, apparently some Christians' behavior led to the accusation that Christianity promoted moral laxity (Rom 3:5-8). So, Paul must address this issue head-on.

He does so, first, by a series of rhetorical questions, with presumed responses, and then by proposing a foundation for his understanding based upon the true nature of baptism into Christ. The mystery of Christian baptism thus forms the backdrop of this passage. Paul addresses baptism in multiple contexts, some of them explicit, others implicit (see 1 Cor 1:13-17; 12:13; Gal 3:26-28). This passage is the longest treatment of the theme of baptism in Paul. This foundation will then allow him to develop his argument further in Romans 7 and 8, showing how the life of faith provides freedom from the Mosaic law and a higher calling to life of the Spirit. The present passage, then, is a key initial statement for Paul's succeeding argumentation.

It should also be noted that Paul virtually personifies Sin. He sees it as a power capable of controlling human life. Sinfulness is not merely a series of evil deeds. In fact, Paul rarely uses the word "sin" (*hamartia*) in the plural. Sin is a controlling power, capable of orienting a person away from God and toward evil. For this reason,

Reflect on the importance of your own baptism. How have you "put it into action"? In what ways do you really practice your faith with conviction?

Most human beings are naturally fearful of death. How does Paul's use of the image of dying with Christ through baptism strike you? What more perhaps needs to "die" in you so that you live out more the hope of the resurrection?

Does Sin feel like an external power that sometimes is operative in your own life? Are there ways to lessen its control? Do you ask the Lord for help in overcoming Sin?

I will capitalize the term (Sin) to emphasize that it is, from Paul's perspective, an independent power whose opposite is found in Christ who gives salvation and new life.

> *We will consider the entire passage a few verses at a time. The occasional questions in the margin (as above) are there for discussion with others. If you are using the materials on your own, use the questions for your own reflection or as a guide to journaling.*

Understanding the Scene

[1]What then shall we say? Shall we persist in sin that grace may abound? Of course not! [2]How can we who died to sin yet live in it? [3]Or are you unaware that we who were baptized into Christ Jesus were baptized into his death? [4]We were indeed buried with him through baptism into death, so that, just as Christ was raised from the dead by the glory of the Father, we too might live in newness of life.

The passage begins with a series of rhetorical questions that help orient Paul's argument. The use of such questions is part of Paul's usual style and is characteristic of Greco-Roman philosophers of the day. Posing such rhetorical questions, or creating imaginary dialogue partners, is what was formally called a *diatribe*. Today the word has come to mean a harangue or belligerent speech. In Paul's day, it meant a style of argumentation.

What is Paul's point? First, his questions respond to the false charge against Christians that their "freedom" from the law leads to moral laxity. Paul strongly responds, "Of course not!" We do not persist in sin in order to provoke God to give more grace. That makes no sense in the Christian mindset. Why? The third and fourth rhetorical questions bring the response. If you have died to Sin, you cannot keep living in it! But

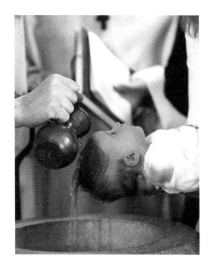

how did we die to Sin? By being baptized! Paul's fourth question rhetorically recalls for his readers their own baptism, the experience of being incorporated into Christ Jesus.

The little preposition "into" (Greek *eis*), used twice in v. 3, does not simply bring to mind the immersion in water that accompanied the rite of baptism. (Recall that the Greek verb *baptizō* means to "immerse.") Rather, it means being truly incorporated into Christ himself, and participating in his death. Paul is obviously speaking in metaphors here, but strong ones. Baptism is a type of death—a death to the power of Sin, which is why Christians cannot simply persist in their sinful habits.

The next verse (v. 4) carries the metaphor further. "We were indeed buried with him through baptism into death . . . ." When you die, you are buried. By baptism, we entered the tomb with Jesus! The very notion of going into the

What does it mean for you to say you are baptized into Christ's death?

tomb with Jesus, who truly experienced death and was indeed buried—as affirmed by the New Testament and the earliest Christian creeds—could seem ghoulish. But Paul's purpose is not to frighten. The main point of this 'death and burial' is *so that* (a strong Greek expression) we might be raised from the dead and live in the newness of life. The actual Greek expression refers to "walking" in newness of life, employing a familiar Old Testament image for the righteous or morally upright life (Prov 8:20; Deut 8:6; Pss 1:1; 15:2; see also 2 Cor 5:7).

Think about what it means to "enter the tomb" with Christ. In what way do you understand that you have entered the tomb with Christ by baptism?

The experience of Christian death in baptism is but a transition to a new life. Paul even uses the opposite preposition of "into" for this expression: "from [Greek *ek*] the dead." Baptism brings about a reversal. We enter Christ's death to share his resurrection. Note, too, that Christ's resurrection is attributed to the "glory of the Father." This recalls the Old Testament image of God's "glory" being the power behind his favorable actions for the Israelites (e.g., Exod 15:7, 11; 16:7, 10). Christ's resurrection is nothing

less than God's gracious action, as he has always performed for his beloved chosen ones from the beginning of creation.

We should note here that Paul's imagery would have likely "rung a bell" with his readers. Using the notion of "death to sin" would have evoked for many of his audience the reality that, for most slaves in the ancient world, the only true freedom came in death. Only when they died could they be liberated and no longer subject to humiliation and mistreatment. Paul conceives of being under the power of Sin as the equivalent of slavery (see v. 6 in the next section). Thus, death to Sin brings about *release* from its power.

⁵For if we have grown into union with him through a death like his, we shall also be united with him in the resurrection. ⁶We know that our old self was crucified with him, so that our sinful body might be done away with, that we might no longer be in slavery to sin. ⁷For a dead person has been absolved from sin. ⁸If, then, we have died with Christ, we believe that we shall also live with him. ⁹We know that Christ, raised from the dead, dies no more; death no longer has power over him. ¹⁰As to his death, he died to sin once and for all; as to his life, he lives for God. ¹¹Consequently, you too must think of yourselves as [being] dead to sin and living for God in Christ Jesus.

Paul now continues his argument, developing it further and then employing the manner of Christ's death (crucifixion) as something Christians participate in by baptism. He reiterates his comparison with Christ's death and resurrection.

We "have grown in union" with Christ by death (through baptism); thus we shall also "be united with him in the resurrection." The Greek expression "grown into" (*symphytoi*) perhaps evokes the image of grafting, which Paul uses elsewhere

when speaking of the Gentiles being grafted onto the "olive tree" of Israel (Rom 11:17-24). By baptism, each Christian grows into Christ, or is grafted onto him.

Paul is utterly confident in the Christian belief in the resurrection, a teaching that of course was difficult for the rationally-oriented Greco-Roman world to comprehend (no less than our own!). But for Paul, and all Christians, this is an essential belief. We participate in Christ's death so as to participate in his eternal life.

Verse 7 is honestly difficult to interpret. The problem is how to understand Paul's use of the verb "has been absolved" (Greek *dedikaiōtai*). It is the same root as Paul's concept of justification or righteousness. Does it mean here being declared innocent or being made righteous or simply being forgiven? It is surely the action of God. The NRSV translates the verse: "For whoever has died is freed from sin." If the exact translation is debatable, the verse can nonetheless be understood. Death brings release from Sin through God's power.

At this point, Paul presents basically the same message, posing a real condition that begins with "If." *If* we have died with Christ (and we have, by baptism), then we believe we will live with him. He goes on to invoke the image of crucifixion—the shameful, humiliating, and excruciating type of death Jesus Christ endured. Paul says, "our old self [literally, "our old human being"] was crucified with him." This is a bold assertion. Obviously, it is not literal but symbolic or metaphorical crucifixion. Paul uses similar potent expressions elsewhere (Gal 2:20) to indicate the strength of his conviction. It is our "old self"—the one associated with our "sinful body"—that died with Christ (by baptism).

We should be careful here not to think of the *sinful body* as referring to sexual sinfulness. The word "body" stands for the whole of our human existence. Though sexual sins are included in the concept, the expression represents the whole of our human finitude. Our humanity is limited, finite, and ultimately under the power of Sin. Yet in baptism it is crucified and buried with Christ, in order to be transformed by the resurrection. Behind the imagery lies Paul's basic understanding that human existence as we know it came from sinful Adam (Rom 5:12-13). But a "new Adam" has come in the person of Christ (Rom 5:14). The old no longer rules; the new has come.

Paul then summarizes and repeats his main points. Dying with Christ means ultimately living with him in an entirely new life. Christian faith affirms that Christ's resurrection means that he can never again experience death. It was

> Paul asserts that our "old self" was crucified with Christ. What is remaining of your "old self" that is yet to be purified by the cross and resurrection?

not a resuscitation or reanimation but a true resurrection or transformation. Once raised from the dead, death is powerless. Christ the Victor can never be subdued again by death. Paul then explains what he means by defining death as death "to sin" *once and for all* (Greek *ephapax*); Christ's own death conquered Sin permanently. Concerning his new *life*, it is a life lived to and for God.

Paul next applies his teaching pastorally for the Romans (and us). "Consequently, you too must think of yourselves as [being] dead to sin and living for God in Christ Jesus." This beautiful expression eloquently joins the two critical elements of Paul's argument: death to Sin, and life unto God through Christ Jesus. The Latin Vulgate version of this verse provides the source of the motto for the community of priests to whom I belong, the Sulpicians: *vivere summe Deo in Christo Jesu* ("To live supremely for God in Christ Jesus"). I can hardly think of a better motto for the Christian life! Note, too, that Paul emphasizes especially that the death is to *Sin*, while the life is *for God through Christ*. Paul is not naïve. He knows that the Roman Christians, as well as all other members of his communities, will still struggle with and succumb to sinful acts; that is still the human condition. It is the vestige of our being descendants from the first Adam. But Sin no longer has control when we put into action our baptismal faith. Christ, the last Adam, has the final word. As Paul will assert in Romans 8, once we die with Christ in baptism, neither Sin nor death have any hold over us (Rom 8:38-39).

Thus, Paul explains the mystery of baptism as participation in Christ's own death and resurrection.

What do I really believe about the resurrection of the dead? Do I live in the hope of the resurrection?

Praying the Word / Sacred Reading

In your imagination, place yourself before the empty tomb of Christ. You are invited to enter. What are your fears and anxieties? By baptism, you have already entered that tomb! How has it transformed you? How have you emerged "on the other side"? What is it like to be "raised from the dead" and to know that death no longer need be feared?

At the end of the exercise, pray the following prayer (or compose one of your own):

Gracious and risen Lord Jesus! I glory in your resurrection, and I give you thanks for calling me forth into the newness of your life.

Walk alongside me, Lord, that I might not lose my way and that I might not succumb to the temptations of Sin. I truly desire to live the life of faith that you have bestowed on me, but I cannot do it alone. Strengthen me with your Holy Spirit.

Lord, teach me also not to fear death and to rejoice rather in the newness of life that you have promised and have already achieved. Energize my faith, Lord, so that I might boldly proclaim your message of hope and joy to all those I meet in the course of my day.

I pray humbly in the confidence of the resurrection, giving thanks to you, the Father, and the Holy Spirit, now and forever. Amen.

Living the Word

Many people live by a kind of "motto" in their lives. It can help keep them focused on a sure path. If you had a motto for your own life, based upon your Christian identity, what would it be? Consider coming up with several possible mottoes that could serve to keep you on a path away from Sin and toward the implementation of your baptismal promises, which we renew every Easter season. (This could be a useful exercise with a group as well.)

Consider volunteering to assist with your local parish program of baptismal preparation.